FOOTBALL SUPERSTARS 2018

JON RICHARDS

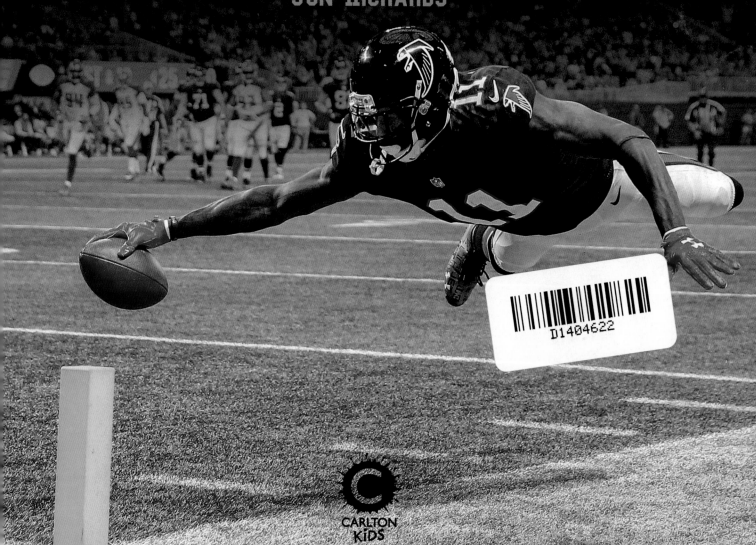

CARLTON KIDS

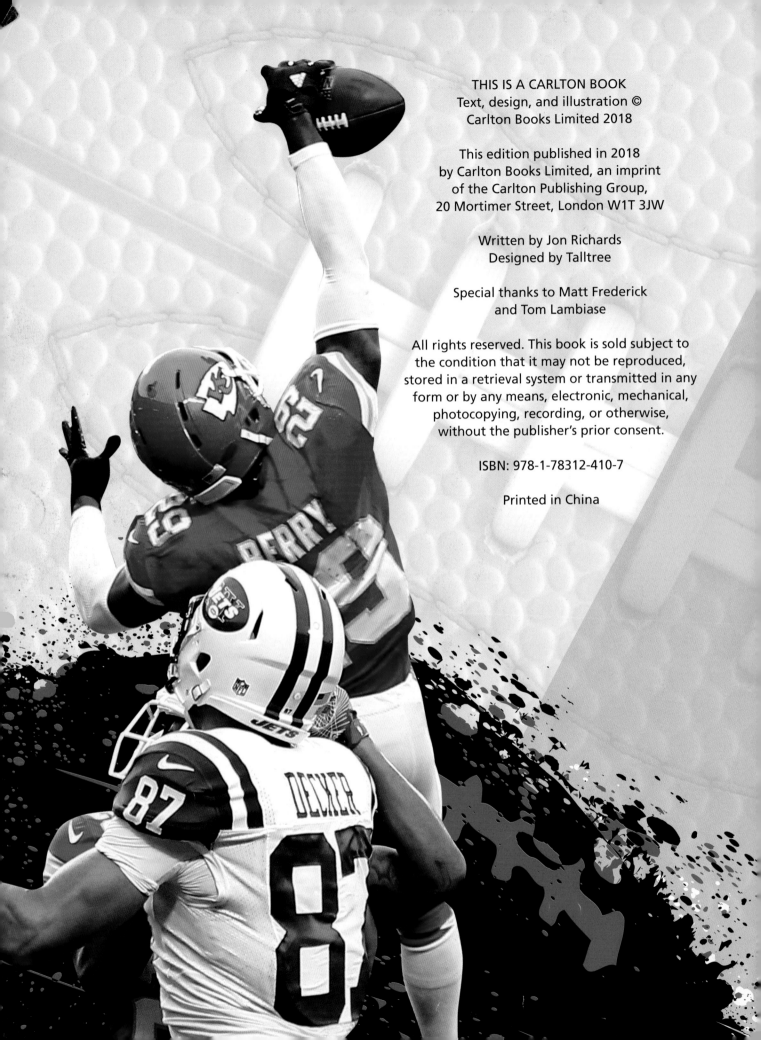

THIS IS A CARLTON BOOK
Text, design, and illustration ©
Carlton Books Limited 2018

This edition published in 2018
by Carlton Books Limited, an imprint
of the Carlton Publishing Group,
20 Mortimer Street, London W1T 3JW

Written by Jon Richards
Designed by Talltree

Special thanks to Matt Frederick
and Tom Lambiase

ISBN: 978-1-78312-410-7

Printed in China

CONTENTS

NOTE TO READERS: THE FACTS AND STATISTICS IN THIS BOOK ARE ACCURATE AS OF FEBRUARY 2018.

NFL 2018 SEASON

This is the **GREATEST COLLECTION** of football talent on the planet! We've chosen the best and **MOST-EXCITING** players from the NFL roster so that you can get the lowdown on their **FACTS**, **STATS**, **STYLE**, and **TECHNIQUE**, and follow their struggle to reach Super Bowl LIII in Atlanta.

NEW YEAR, NEW SEASON

With preseason warm-ups out of the way, the hard work starts on September 6, with the NFL Kickoff game hosted by new champions, the Philadelphia Eagles. Over the next 17 weeks, the 32 teams that make up the NFL's six divisions slug it out for a chance to reach the playoffs on the road to Super Bowl glory. On the way, the NFL is taking the show far and wide. Its International Series sees three games in London, UK, where the Raiders face the Seahawks, the Jaguars host the Eagles, and the Chargers come up against the Titans. There's also a game at the famous Azteca Stadium in Mexico City, Mexico, where the Rams will host the Chiefs.

EYES ON THE PRIZE

This season promises as much, if not more, excitement as the last one. Can the Eagles repeat their shock win and clinch a second Super Bowl? Will Tom Brady (left) steer the Patriots to success this time, making them one of the sport's most successful teams of all time? Can Drew Brees guide the Steelers back to the top, or will fellow veteran Eli Manning and the Giants beat them to it in the NFC? Or is there another surprise team lurking in the shadows, ready to steal the thunder?

GET READY TO RUMBLE!

It's going to be an exciting 2018 season, as the regular season leads to Wild Cards, followed by the Divisional round, which leads to the Conference championships, and then on to the Super Bowl itself, where quarterback Nick Foles will be hoping to repeat his victory with the Eagles. Whatever happens, fans are guaranteed an action-packed ride filled with the thrills and spills that come with top-level, hard-hitting football.

AARON RODGERS

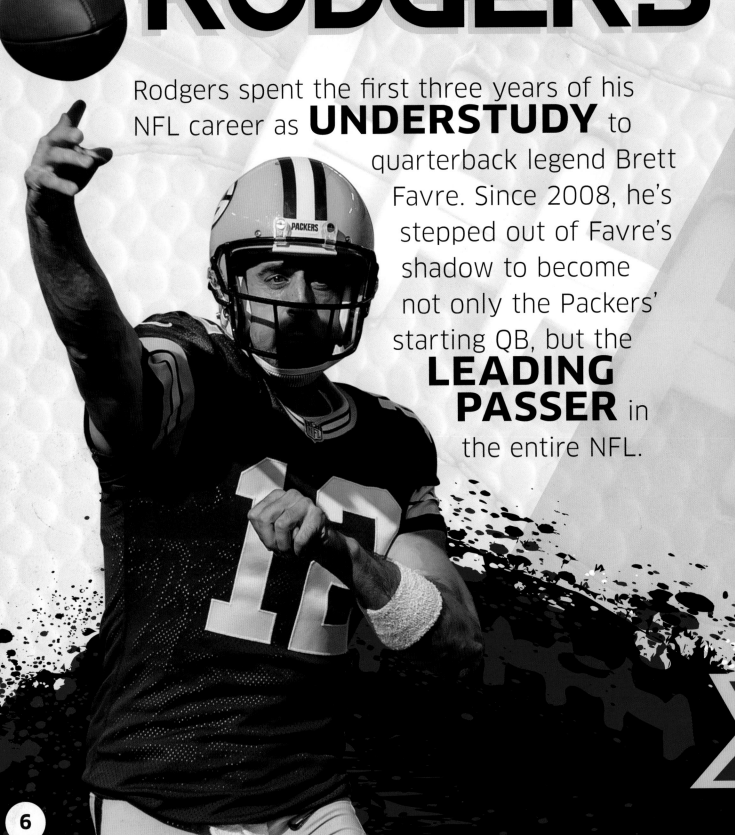

Rodgers spent the first three years of his NFL career as **UNDERSTUDY** to quarterback legend Brett Favre. Since 2008, he's stepped out of Favre's shadow to become not only the Packers' starting QB, but the **LEADING PASSER** in the entire NFL.

GREEN BAY PACKERS | QUARTERBACK

D.O.B: DECEMBER 2, 1983 | **HEIGHT:** 6'2" | **WEIGHT:** 225 LBS
DEBUT: vs. NEW ORLEANS SAINTS, OCTOBER 9, 2005 (3–52 WIN)
GAMES: 149 | **ATT:** 4,895 | **COMP:** 3,188 | **YARDS:** 38,502 | **TDS:** 313

RECORD BREAKER

Rodgers has made a habit of setting and breaking records throughout his football career. At school, he set passing records for single games and across the season. Despite this, he failed to attract the attention of a college and even considered giving up football to concentrate on law. Fortunately, he was discovered by the University of California Golden Bears and had two successful seasons with them. Declaring himself available for the 2005 NFL Draft, Rodgers was expected to be picked early on, ideally by the team he had supported as a boy, the 49ers. Instead, the 49ers went elsewhere, and Rodgers had a nervous wait before the Packers made him the 24th pick.

INTO THE LIMELIGHT

Serving as Favre's understudy gave Rodgers the chance to perfect his game, and he soon earned a reputation for working the practice squads too hard! In 2008, Rodgers finally got his chance to shine and he didn't disappoint, guiding the Packers to the playoffs and putting together the third-longest run of consecutive pass attempts without an interception (157). Two years later, Rodgers went even further, steering the Packers all the way to the Super Bowl. At Super Bowl XLV against the Steelers, Rodgers threw for 304 yards and three touchdowns in the 31–25 win, and was voted Super Bowl MVP.

QUARTERBACK STAR

Super Bowl Champion, two-time NFL MVP, six-time Pro Bowl player, two-time NFL passer rating leader, highest passer rating in a season (122.5), highest passer rating in a career (103.8)—Rodgers has achieved it all during his career with the Packers. And he's not over yet. In 2016, he led the league with 40 touchdown passes, but his 2017 season was limited to just seven games after a broken collar-bone needed 13 screws to hold it together.

Rodgers jumps in to congratulate tight end Martellus Bennett after a successful touchdown pass against the Redskins in August 2017.

>>>>> FAST FACT >>>>>
Rodgers has *the best touchdown-to-interception ratio in NFL history, with an average of 4.13 touchdowns for every interception thrown!*

PATRICK PETERSON

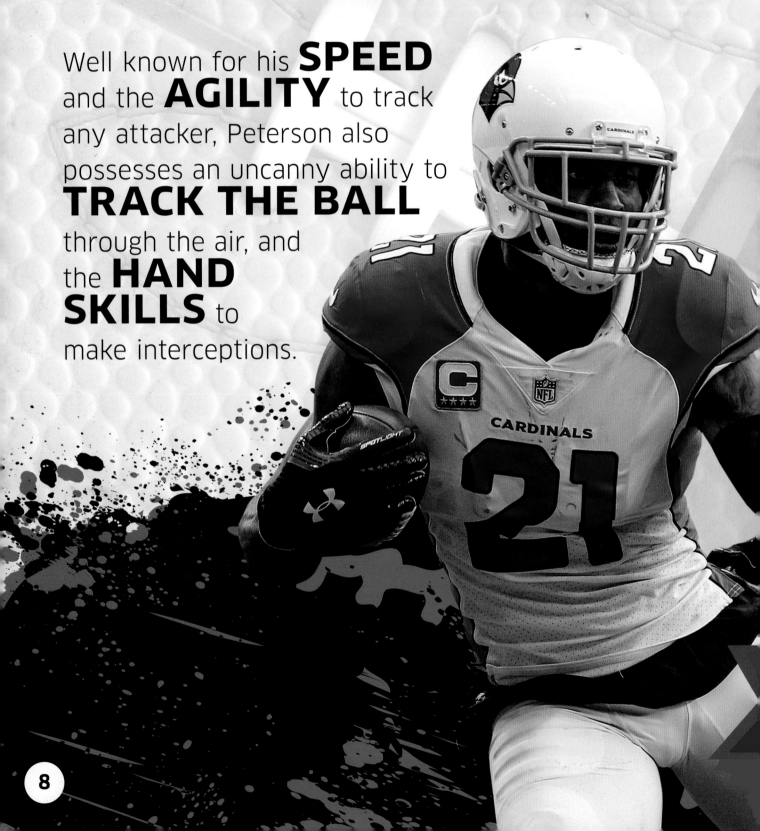

Well known for his **SPEED** and the **AGILITY** to track any attacker, Peterson also possesses an uncanny ability to **TRACK THE BALL** through the air, and the **HAND SKILLS** to make interceptions.

ARIZONA CARDINALS | CORNERBACK

D.O.B: JULY 11, 1990 | **HEIGHT:** 6'1" | **WEIGHT:** 203 LBS
DEBUT: vs. CAROLINA PANTHERS, SEPTEMBER 11, 2011 (28–21 WIN)
GAMES: 112 | **TACKLES:** 331 | **SACKS:** 2.0 | **INT:** | **TDS:** 1

SCHOOL AND COLLEGE

Growing up in Florida, Peterson played high school football for the Blanche Ely Mighty Tigers where he excelled as a defensive back and a running back. In his senior year, he recorded 733 yards for 11 touchdowns, as well as 21 tackles and five interceptions. His performances on the field led to *USA Today* naming him Defensive Player of the Year. He chose to attend LSU and continued with his incredible form, winning the Jim Thorpe Award in 2010 for the nation's top defensive back, and was twice selected First-team All-American. Leaving college after his junior year, many expected him to be an early pick in the 2011 NFL Draft.

CARDINALS CORNERBACK

The Cardinals chose Peterson as their first round pick in the Draft (fifth overall) and immediately made him their starting cornerback. In the season opener against the Panthers, he scored his first career touchdown when he returned a punt for 89 yards to win the game 28–21. He ended his first season by becoming the only rookie chosen for the 2011 All-Pro First Team and he was also selected for the Pro Bowl, an achievement he's since repeated for every one of his seven seasons with the NFL.

PEAK PERFORMANCE

Peterson has played in every single regular season game in his seven seasons with the Cardinals, largely as cornerback and punt returner. He's also had stints as a running back, kick returner, wide receiver, and, in 2013, he posted his one and only pass, a successful completion for 17 yards. In the process, he became the first defensive player to catch and complete a pass in the same game since the merger of the leagues.

Peterson grabs a pass meant for Falcons' wide receiver Taylor Gabriel during a preseason game in August 2017.

>>>>> FAST FACT >>>>>

***Peterson** holds two NFL records—the most punt return touchdowns in a single season, with four, and also for the longest overtime punt return touchdown of 99 yards.*

A.J. GREEN

He may not be the **BIGGEST PLAYER** on the field, but what he lacks in **SIZE**, A. J. Green more than makes up for in **SPEED**, jump height, and the ability to **PULL IN** the most poorly thrown pass.

GREEN
18

CINCINNATI BENGALS | WIDE RECEIVER

D.O.B: JULY 31, 1988 | **HEIGHT:** 6'4" | **WEIGHT:** 210 LBS
DEBUT: vs. CLEVELAND BROWNS, SEPTEMBER 11, 2011 (27–17 WIN)
GAMES: 102 | **RECEPTIONS:** 556 | **YARDS:** 8,213 | **TDS:** 57

EARLY PROSPECT

Green proved to be a high school star not just on the football field, but also the basketball court and the athletics track. He was part of the team that won the 2007–2008 South Carolina high school state championship and he also competed in track and field as a long jumper and triple jumper. His ability on the football field, however, drew the attention of national press and some analysts predicted that he would be appearing in the NFL by 2011. He moved to the University of Georgia and finished his first year there by setting freshman records for number of catches (56), yards (963), and touchdowns (eight).

ROARING BENGAL

Green carried his form right through college, finishing his three years there with 166 receptions for 2,619 yards and 23 touchdowns before he opted to enter the 2011 NFL Draft. The Bengals were quick to pick him up, signing him to a four-year, $19.6 million contract. In his first year at Cincinnati he formed a valuable partnership with fellow rookie QB Andy Dalton, and the two set new Bengals rookie records for yards and receptions. Green also finished that year with more receptions and receiving yards than any other NFL rookie that season.

MISTER CONSISTENCY

In his seven seasons with the Bengals, Green has continued to perform at the highest level. The 2013 season proved to be one high point as he finished the year with career highs of 98 receptions for 1,426 yards (the second-highest total yardage in the Bengals' history). This consistency has been rewarded by selection to the Pro Bowl in every one of those seven seasons. In fact, he's only had one season (2016) where he failed to reach 1,000 yards receiving, and that was only because a torn hamstring limited the number of games he played to just ten that year!

Green celebrates scoring a touchdown against the Bears with fellow wide receiver Brandon LaFell in December 2017.

>>>>> FAST FACT >>>>>

At school, *Green took up juggling, and was even part of his elementary school juggling team. He claims that he could juggle up to four items at once.*

TOM BRADY

The **STATS** don't lie, and it's hard to argue with Tom Brady's **FIGURES**. No one has won more **SUPER BOWL RINGS**, and despite missing out on Super Bowl LII, he's ready to guide the Patriots on another successful **TITLE CHARGE**.

BRADY
12

NEW ENGLAND PATRIOTS | QUARTERBACK

D.O.B: AUGUST 3, 1977 | **HEIGHT:** 6'4" | **WEIGHT:** 225 LBS
DEBUT: vs. DETROIT LIONS, NOVEMBER 23, 2000 (34–9 LOSS)
GAMES: 253 | **ATT:** 8,805 | **COMP:** 5,629 | **YARDS:** 66,159 | **TDS:** 488

TOUGH START

It's hard to believe it now, but Brady had a tough start to his football career. Growing up in California, he was only a backup quarterback for his high school to begin with and struggled to get noticed by colleges. He was offered a contract to play Major League Baseball with the Montreal Expos, but he turned the offer down to pursue his first love—football. Brady joined the University of Michigan and was backup quarterback for his first two seasons before battling his way to the starting role. In the 2000 NFL Draft, he had to wait until the sixth round and the 199th pick overall before he was chosen by the Patriots in what many analysts now call the biggest "steal" in NFL Draft History.

THE WINNINGEST

In his first season with the Patriots, Brady was backup QB again, this time to Drew Bledsoe. In fact, he only managed one completion throughout the 2000 season! The following year, Brady stepped into the limelight when Bledsoe was injured, leading the Patriots to victory over the Rams in Super Bowl XXXVI, and picking up a Super Bowl MVP as well. Since he took over as starting QB, the Patriots have never posted a losing season, picking up 14 division titles and eight AFC Championships on the way. Brady and Patriots' Head Coach Bill Belichick have formed the most successful head coach-quarterback duo in NFL history.

SIMPLY THE BEST?

The list of NFL records held by Brady is as long as they come. He's won more games than any other starting quarterback (regular season, playoffs, and Super Bowl), has thrown the most touchdown passes in a Super Bowl (18), has attempted the most passes in a single Super Bowl (62), completed the most passes in a Super Bowl (43), and has the most passing yards in the Playoffs (10,226)—no wonder people rate him the best there's ever been!

Brady marshalls the Patriots' offensive line against the Steelers in December 2017.

>>>>> **FAST FACT** >>>>>
In the 16 years *that Brady has started for the New England Patriots, he has guided the team to eight Super Bowl appearances, more than any other player.*

AARON DONALD

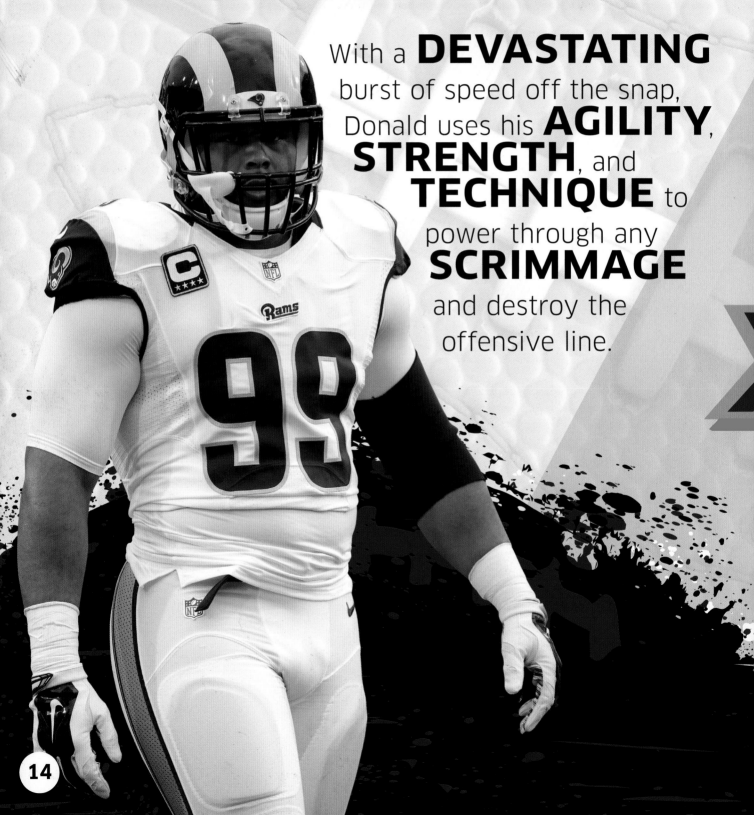

With a **DEVASTATING** burst of speed off the snap, Donald uses his **AGILITY**, **STRENGTH**, and **TECHNIQUE** to power through any **SCRIMMAGE** and destroy the offensive line.

DONALD 99

LOS ANGELES RAMS | DEFENSIVE TACKLE

D.O.B: MAY 23, 1991 | **HEIGHT:** 6'1" | **WEIGHT:** 280 LBS
DEBUT: vs. MINNESOTA VIKINGS, SEPTEMBER 7, 2014 (34–6 LOSS)
GAMES: 62 | **TACKLES:** 205 | **SACKS:** 39.0

CLOSE TO HOME

Growing up in Pittsburgh, Donald excelled on the football field while still in high school, posting 63 tackles, 15 tackles for loss, and 11 sacks. Despite offers from several colleges, he chose to stay close to home and attend the University of Pittsburgh. Throughout his college career, his performances improved year-on-year and he ended his senior season with 59 tackles, 28.5 tackles for loss, 11 sacks, and four forced fumbles. He was also picked as ACC Defensive Player of the Year and made a unanimous All-American.

A GOOD START

Donald was picked by the Rams in the first round (13th overall) in the 2014 NFL Draft, who offered him a $10.13 million four-year contract, including a $5.69 million signing bonus. He played in all 16 of the Rams' regular season games, posting 47 tackles, nine sacks, and two forced fumbles. His performance saw him selected for the Pro Bowl and he was even voted NFL Defensive Rookie of the Year. For 2015, Donald was made starting defensive tackle and started the season with a bang, recording a career-high nine tackles against the Seahawks in the season opener. That year, his figures were even better than his rookie season, and he recorded 69 tackles, 11 sacks, a defended pass, and a fumble recovery.

>>>>> FAST FACT >>>>>

At the NFL Combine in 2014, Donald posted the fastest time ever recorded in a 40-yard dash for a defensive tackle with 4.69 seconds.

Saints quarterback, Drew Brees, feels the force of a Donald sack in a game at the Los Angeles Memorial Coliseum in November 2017.

DEFENSIVE STAR

Last year proved to be Donald's stellar season. Despite missing the first game following a contract dispute, he still managed to record 41 tackles, 11 sacks, and five forced fumbles. He was picked for the Pro Bowl for a fourth consecutive year and was named a first-team All-Pro for the third time. On the back of this, he was chosen as the Defensive Player of the Year. With his career on the up, 2018 promises to be an even better one for the Rams' defense.

LUKE KUECHLY

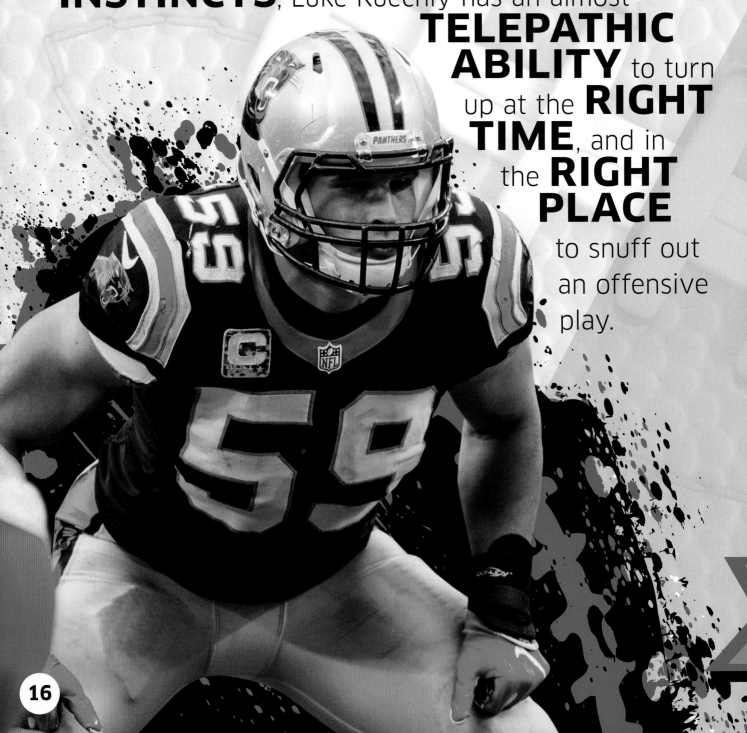

Technically sound and with amazing football **INSTINCTS**, Luke Kuechly has an almost **TELEPATHIC ABILITY** to turn up at the **RIGHT TIME**, and in the **RIGHT PLACE** to snuff out an offensive play.

KUECHLY
59

CAROLINA PANTHERS | MIDDLE LINEBACKER

D.O.B: APRIL 20, 1991 | **HEIGHT:** 6'3" | **WEIGHT:** 238 LBS
DEBUT: vs. TAMPA BAY BUCCANEERS, SEPTEMBER 9, 2012 (10–16 LOSS)
GAMES: 86 | **TACKLES:** 818 | **SACKS:** 10.5 | **INT:** 15 | **TDS:** 1

COLLEGE SENSATION

Kuechly excelled at college football, playing for the Boston College Eagles. He became starting outside linebacker in his freshman year and finished the season with 158 tackles (87 solo tackles), which were the highest in the team and the conference, and second highest in the whole country. He went even better in his sophomore year, posting 183 tackles (110 solo), the best in the nation, and had a 21-game streak where he made at least 10 tackles per game. His junior year was better still—he made 191 tackles (102 solo tackles) at an average of 16 tackles per game, breaking the team and conference tackling records he had only set the year before, and winning the 2011 Butkus Award for the best college linebacker.

PLAYER OF THE YEAR

Kuechly entered the 2012 NFL Draft as one of the highest ranked linebackers. The Panthers were quick to pounce and made him their first-round pick (9th overall). Starting off as outside linebacker, Kuechly was soon moved to middle linebacker to cover for injuries and finished that year with a huge 164 tackles. The next year proved even better. He played a key role in a superb Panthers defense which finished second in the league for yards and points allowed. For his performances that year, Kuechly was voted NFL Defensive Player of the Year.

CATCHING MACHINE

Throughout the 2014 season, Kuechly continued his awesome form. So much so, that the Panthers offered him a five-year $62 million extension in 2015, making him the highest paid middle linebacker in the NFL by average annual salary. Kuechly backed up these figures by helping the team all the way to Super Bowl 50 (they dropped the Roman numerals for that year!) where they were defeated 24–10 by the Denver Broncos. The next couple of seasons were hampered by injury, but that didn't stop Kuechly posting incredible figures and in 2017, he finished with 125 tackles (74 solo tackles) and was selected for his fifth straight Pro Bowl appearance.

Kuechly tackles Saints' running back Alvin Kamara during a game in December 2017, which the Saints went on to win 31–21.

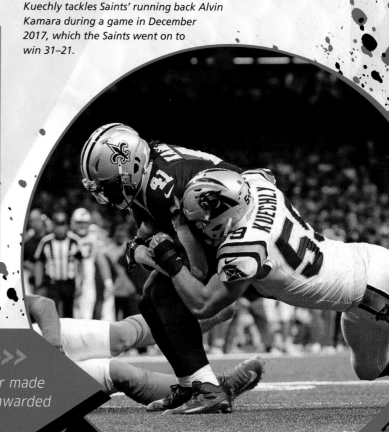

>>>>> FAST FACT >>>>>

Kuechly was the third youngest player ever made NFL Defensive Rookie of the Year when he was awarded the title after his first season.

MATT RYAN

Matt Ryan is one of the most accurate **PASSERS** in the modern game. With a completion rate of nearly **65 PERCENT** during his ten seasons with the Falcons, it's little wonder that, in 2016, he was voted **NFL PLAYER OF THE YEAR**.

ATLANTA FALCONS | QUARTERBACK

D.O.B: MAY 17, 1985 | **HEIGHT:** 6'4" | **WEIGHT:** 217 LBS
DEBUT: vs. DETROIT LIONS, SEPTEMBER 7, 2008 (21–34 WIN)
GAMES: 158 | **ATT:** 5,593 | **COMP:** 3,630 | **YARDS:** 41,796 | **TDS:** 260

SCHOOL AND COLLEGE

Ryan proved himself an all-around athlete in high school and was captain of his football, basketball, AND baseball teams. He was an accomplished small forward on the basketball court and played as pitcher and shortstop on the baseball team, but it was as a quarterback that he excelled and during his senior year, he threw for 1,300 yards. He continued his throwing form into college and led the Boston College Eagles on what was the nation's longest bowl winning streak during his senior year, when he also won the Johnny Unitas Golden Arm Award for the country's most outstanding senior quarterback.

GOLDEN ARM

In 2008, Ryan was drafted third overall by the Falcons and signed a $72 million six-year contract, making him the fourth highest paid quarterback in the NFL—even though he hadn't played a single professional game! He immediately became the Falcons' starting quarterback and made an immediate impact by throwing his first NFL pass for a 62-yard touchdown! His best year to date came in 2016 when he finished the regular season posting a career best yardage of 4,944 from 534 attempts and a completion rate of 69.9 percent. He also led the Falcons to Super Bowl LI, where they lost in overtime to the Patriots.

UNDER PRESSURE

In college, Ryan earned a reputation for staying calm when opposition defenses tried to put on the pressure. He's just as happy (and accurate) when he's on the move out of the pocket and is more than capable of taking punishment from opposition linebackers. His consistent form over ten years in the NFL has seen him win NFL Offensive Rookie of the Year (2008), NFL Offensive Player of the Year (2016), and taken him to four Pro Bowls.

Ryan controls the offensive line during the NFC Wildcard game against the Los Angeles Rams in January 2018.

>>>>> FAST FACT >>>>>

At the end of the 2017 season, Ryan set the record for the most passing yards over ten seasons with 41,796, breaking the record set by Peyton Manning.

KHALIL MACK

When he's not **SMASHING** through an offensive line, Khalil Mack is hunting down runners and quarterbacks. Still new to the NFL, he's already made three **PRO BOWLS** and, in 2017, his fellow players voted him the **HIGHEST-RANKED** defensive lineman.

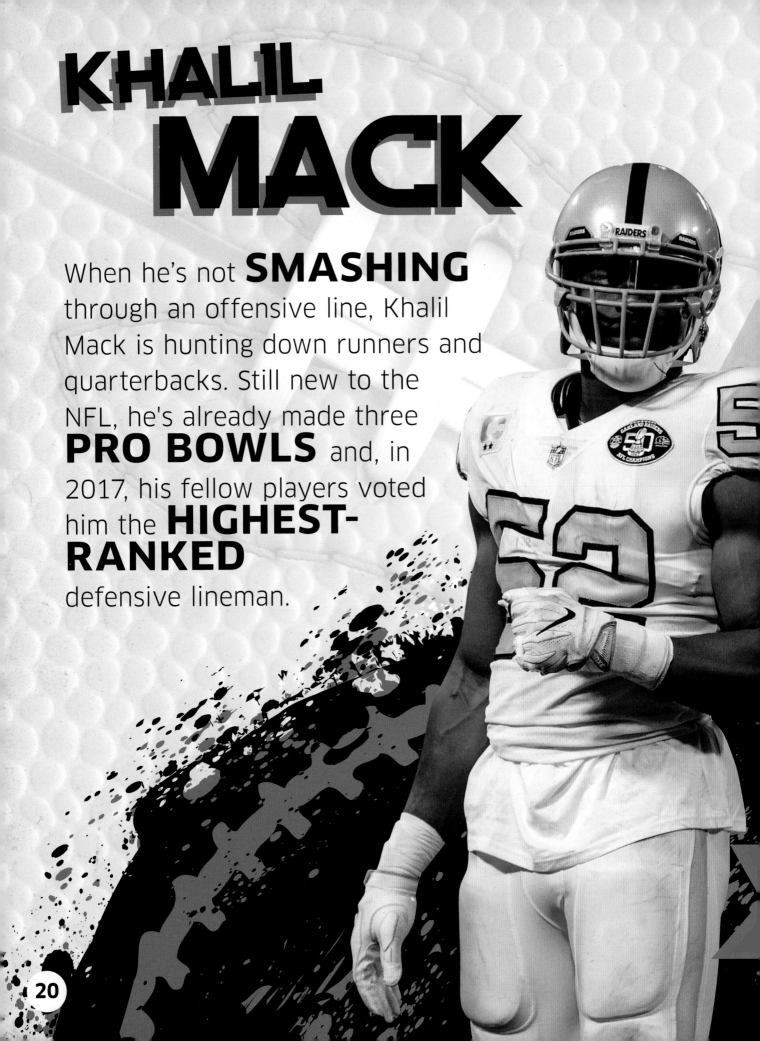

MACK
52

OAKLAND RAIDERS | DEFENSIVE END

D.O.B: FEBRUARY 22, 1991 | **HEIGHT:** 6'3" | **WEIGHT:** 250 LBS
DEBUT: vs. NEW YORK JETS, SEPTEMBER 7, 2014 (14–19 LOSS)
GAMES: 64 | **TACKLES:** 304 | **SACKS:** 40.5

SPORTING START

In school, Mack's first love was basketball, and his hopes for a college scholarship lay with that sport. But his hoop dreams were shattered by a tear to a knee tendon. Thankfully, his high school football coach persuaded Mack that gridiron was the way forward, and his performances in the defensive line earned him a place at the State University of New York in Buffalo. After redshirting in his freshman year, Mack's college career really took off and in his senior year he recorded 100 tackles, 19 tackles for loss, 10.5 sacks, and three interceptions (one for a touchdown). He also set an NCAA record for forced fumbles with 16.

BOMBSHELL MAN

For such a destructive defensive end, it might be surprising to learn that Mack started his career on the other side of the scrimmage—as a quarterback! At high school, this talented playmaker had the nickname "Bombshell Man," but issues with his passing game saw him switch to defense—and he never looked back! His speed from a standing start can be devastating, his pass-rush game is second to none, and he uses his pace to chase down ball carriers. And when he strikes you'd better watch out! His tackle technique sees him hit low and up, driving the ball carrier backward and frequently knocking the ball clean out of his hands.

Mack tries to blast his way through the Cowboys' offensive line during a preseason game in August 2017.

TO THE NFL

With the figures he was posting in college, it's no surprise that Mack was touted for big things in the pro game. In the 2014 NFL Draft, he was picked fifth overall by the Raiders and he didn't disappoint his new bosses. In his rookie season, he blew away opposition offenses, recording 76 tackles, four sacks, and one forced fumble. In only his second season, he was picked for the Pro Bowl, and in 2016, he was instrumental in helping the Raiders reach the playoffs for the first time since 2002.

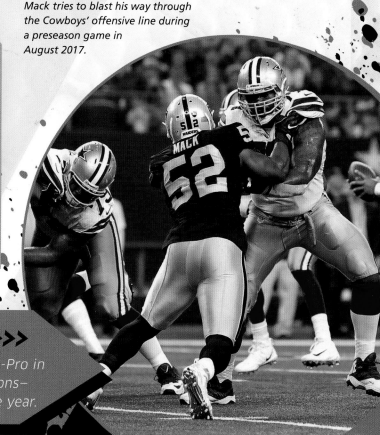

>>>>> FAST FACT >>>>>

In 2015, Mack became the first first-team All-Pro in NFL history to be elected to two different positions—defensive end and outside linebacker—in the same year.

21

VON MILLER

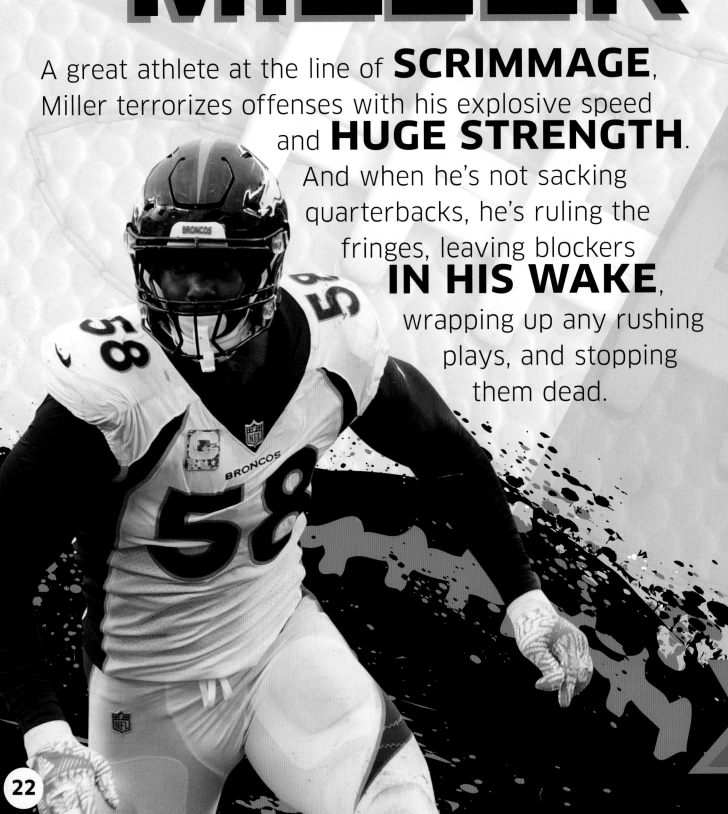

A great athlete at the line of **SCRIMMAGE**, Miller terrorizes offenses with his explosive speed and **HUGE STRENGTH**. And when he's not sacking quarterbacks, he's ruling the fringes, leaving blockers **IN HIS WAKE**, wrapping up any rushing plays, and stopping them dead.

DENVER BRONCOS | OUTSIDE LINEBACKER

D.O.B: MARCH 26, 1989 | **HEIGHT:** 6'3" | **WEIGHT:** 250 LBS
DEBUT: vs. OAKLAND RAIDERS, SEPTEMBER 12, 2011 (23–20 LOSS)
GAMES: 104 | **TACKLES:** 395 | **SACKS:** 83.5

SCHOOL AND COLLEGE

At DeSoto High School, Texas, Miller excelled in the defensive line, recording 76 tackles and six sacks during his senior year. He also made his mark at track and field, taking part in the 110-meter hurdles, the triple jump, and the javelin. Needless to say he drew the attention of several major colleges, including Florida and Oklahoma, but went with Texas A&M and the Aggies. He saw the chance to join the NFL draft in 2010, but chose to stay on for his senior year, when a superb season saw him win the Butkus Award as the nation's best college linebacker. He graduated in 2011 with a degree in poultry science and even raises chickens in his spare time!

FLYING START

Miller was picked second in the 2011 NFL draft and made an immediate impression in the regular season. In his very first play from scrimmage against the Oakland Raiders, he forced a fumble and recorded his first NFL sack just six days later against the Bengals. He finished the season with 11.5 sacks, 19 quarterback hits, and 29 quarterback hurries, which led to him being named AP Defensive Rookie of the Year and a spot at the 2012 Pro Bowl. The next season, he carried on where he left off, grabbing ten sacks in just nine games.

TOP ROOKIE

The 2015 season proved a huge high point in Miller's career. He became the third fastest player to reach 50 sacks, taking just 58 games to achieve the feat. He played a key role in the Broncos' run to the Super Bowl, recording 2.5 sacks against the Patriots' Tom Brady in the AFC Championship. In Super Bowl 50, the Broncos came up against the much-favored Panthers, but in the first quarter, Miller sacked Panthers' quarterback Cam Newton, and knocked the ball free which was scooped up by fellow Bronco Malik Johnson for a fumble return touchdown. Later in the game, Miller stepped up again, forcing another fumble from Newton deep in the fourth quarter to snuff out any hopes of a Panthers' victory.

Miller applies some pressure to Redskins' quarterback Kirk Cousins during the last game of the 2017 regular season.

>>>>> FAST FACT >>>>>

In 2016, *Miller appeared on "Dancing with the Stars," partnering professional dancer Witney Carson. He finished the competition in 8th place.*

CARSON WENTZ

TALL, athletic, and with a strong, accurate arm, Carson Wentz is one of the most exciting **QUARTERBACKS** on the NFL roster. And he's been influential in turning the Eagles into a team of **WORLD CHAMPIONS**.

WENTZ
11

PHILADELPHIA EAGLES | CARSON WENTZ

D.O.B: DECEMBER 30, 1992 | **HEIGHT:** 6'5" | **WEIGHT:** 237 LBS
DEBUT: vs. CLEVELAND BROWNS, SEPTEMBER 11, 2016 (10–29 WIN)
GAMES: 29 | **ATT:** 1,047 | **COMP:** 644 | **YARDS:** 7,078 | **TDS:** 49

PASSING AND RUSHING

Moving with his family to North Dakota at the age of three, Wentz played football, basketball, and baseball for his high school team. In 2011, he moved to North Dakota State University, where he redshirted his first year. The next two years he spent as backup quarterback on the team, before making the starting lineup during his junior year in 2014. In that season, he started all 16 games, leading NDSU to a 15–1 record, completing 228 of 358 passes for 3,111 yards and 25 touchdowns. He was also the team's second leading rusher with 642 yards and six touchdowns.

IMMEDIATE STARTER

Wentz was thrown into the starting lineup for the Eagles right away, and he didn't disappoint. He led them to a 29–10 victory over the Browns in his very first game, throwing for 278 yards and two touchdowns. He started all 16 games of his first regular season setting a new NFL record for most pass completions by a rookie with 379. The following year was brought to an end by a knee injury in week 14, but that didn't stop him posting Eagles' records for touchdown passes in a single season (33). He was forced to sit out the rest of the season and the Eagles' march to Super Bowl glory.

INTO THE NFL

His senior year at college was cut short by a broken wrist against South Dakota—but not before he'd finished the game recording 195 passing yards and two touchdown passes. He came back for the national championships later that year leading the NDSU Bison to its fifth straight FCS title. His abilities to command an offense led many analysts and experts to regard him as a high-level pick in the 2016 NFL Draft. This was proved correct when the Eagles picked the QB in the very first round and second overall, signing him up to a four-year $26.67 million contract, including a $17.6 million signing bonus.

Wentz holds the Vince Lombardi Trophy after the Eagles' stunning victory over the Patriots in Super Bowl LII.

>>>>> FAST FACT >>>>>

As a freshman in high school, Wentz was only 5'8" tall, but by the time he had graduated to college he had grown to 6'5" tall!

25

ANTONIO BROWN

With six **PRO BOWL** appearances, more than 9,000 yards, and 59 touchdowns, Antonio Brown is now firmly established as one of the NFL's most potent **OFFENSIVE THREATS**, whether it's plucking passes out of the air or **RETURNING PUNTS** deep into enemy territory.

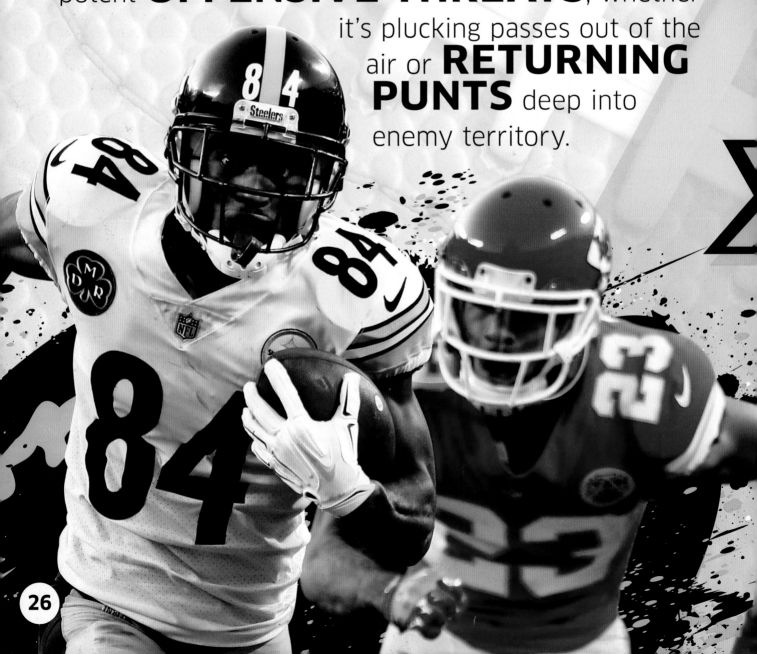

PITTSBURGH STEELERS | WIDE RECEIVER

D.O.B: JULY 10, 1988 | **HEIGHT:** 5'10" | **WEIGHT:** 181 LBS
DEBUT: vs. TENNESSEE TITANS, SEPTEMBER 19, 2010 (19–11 WIN)
GAMES: 115 | **RECEPTIONS:** 733 | **YARDS:** 9,910

FOOTBALL TALENT

In high school, Brown excelled at football, playing running back, quarterback, wide receiver, and punt returner. He also turned his amazing pace to the track, running in the 100-meter dash and as part of the 4 x 100 meter relay. After school, he moved from North Carolina Tech, and won a scholarship to Florida International University, but was expelled before he had a chance to attend. He ended up at Central Michigan and over three seasons he posted 305 receptions for 3,199 yards and 22 touchdowns.

TOUGH START

Brown decided to forego his senior year, making himself available for the 2010 NFL Draft. He was chosen by the Steelers in the sixth round (195th overall) and won a place on the squad as the fifth wide receiver. During his first season, he only played in nine games, making 16 catches. Over the next few years, Brown worked his way up the list. In his second NFL season, he became the first player ever to record more than 1,000 yards both receiving and returning. By 2013, he was a starting wide receiver and during that year he became the only receiver in history to record five catches, and at least 50 yards, in every game of an NFL season.

Brown shows his trademark athleticism to pluck the ball out of the air during a preseason game against the Colts in August 2017.

>>>>> FAST FACT >>>>>

Brown is the son of retired Arena Football League star Eddie Brown, who many people rate as the best Arena football player of all time.

TOP EARNER

During his NFL career, Brown has attracted the attention of the game's lawmakers, and has been fined for unsportsmanlike behavior, excessive celebration, and even for wearing baby blue cleats! But that hasn't stopped his record-breaking performances on the field. In both the 2014 and the 2017 seasons, he led the league for most yards, posting 1,698 and 1,533 yards respectively. His reward? In February 2017, the Steelers offered him a new five-year contract extension worth $68 million, with $19 million guaranteed at signing and a $17 million annual price tag, making Brown the highest paid wide receiver in the NFL.

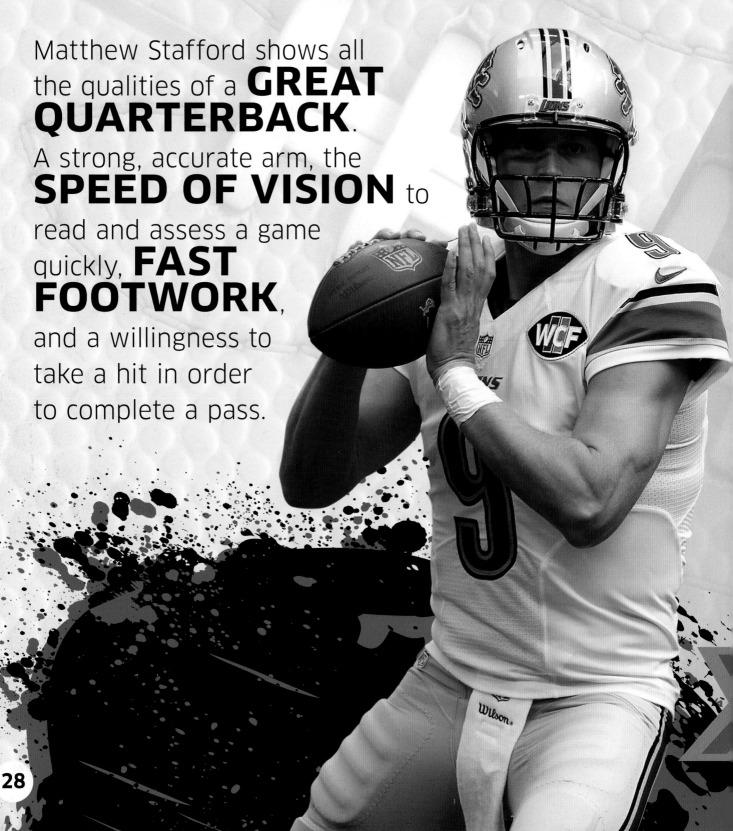

MATTHEW STAFFORD

Matthew Stafford shows all the qualities of a **GREAT QUARTERBACK**. A strong, accurate arm, the **SPEED OF VISION** to read and assess a game quickly, **FAST FOOTWORK**, and a willingness to take a hit in order to complete a pass.

STAFFORD
9

DETROIT LIONS | QUARTERBACK

D.O.B: FEBRUARY 7, 1988 | **HEIGHT:** 6'3" | **WEIGHT:** 220 LBS
DEBUT: vs. NEW ORLEANS SAINTS, SEPTEMBER 13, 2009 (27–45 LOSS)
GAMES: 125 | **ATT:** 4,850 | **COMP:** 3,005 | **YARDS:** 34,749 | **TDS:** 216

ONE TO WATCH

Early on in his football career, Stafford was singled out by experts as a potential star of the future. In fact, before he'd even played a game at college level, football analyst Mel Kiper, Jr. said that the young quarterback would be the "Number One pick in the NFL Draft." His form at college level for the Georgia Bulldogs drew the attention of NFL franchise scouts. Unsurprisingly, he elected not to stay on for his senior year, making himself available for the 2009 NFL Draft, where the Lions chose him as their number one choice, and the number one pick overall, bringing true Mel Kiper, Jr.'s prediction made three years earlier!

PASSING MACHINE

Stafford established himself in the Lions' starting lineup from his very first game—and has remained there ever since. In one game during his first season in 2009, he defied doctors' instructions after separating a shoulder and returned to the field to throw a game-winning pass in a 38–37 victory over the Cleveland Browns. Since then, the form of the Lions has been varied, reaching the playoffs for just three seasons, but Stafford's form has remained consistent. It's no wonder, then, that the Lions offered their star quarterback an enormous five-year contract extension of $135 million, making him the highest-paid player in NFL history to date.

RECORD BREAKER

Stafford holds an impressive list of NFL quarterback records. These include the most passing touchdowns in a single game by a rookie, with five (he also became the youngest to achieve this feat), the most games in a season with at least one touchdown pass (16 in 2011), the most fourth quarter comebacks in a season (8 in 2016), the most passing attempts in a season (727 in 2012), the fastest player to reach 3,000 completions (125 games played), and the first player in NFL history to complete 60% or more of all passes in every game of a season (2015).

Not afraid to rush when required, Stafford takes on the Seahawks defense during the playoffs in January 2017.

>>>>> FAST FACT >>>>>

Stafford is the fastest player in NFL history to throw for 30,000 yards, taking just 109 games to reach this historic milestone.

JALEN RAMSEY

Using his champion track and field speed, Ramsey hunts down opponents, disrupting **OFFENSIVE PLAYS** with a lightning-quick change of direction. His incredible jumping ability means he can **OUT-LEAP** many wide receivers to **DEFLECT** or **INTERCEPT** an incoming pass.

JACKSONVILLE JAGUARS | CORNERBACK

D.O.B: OCTOBER 24, 1994 | **HEIGHT:** 6'1" | **WEIGHT:** 208 LBS
DEBUT: vs. GREEN BAY PACKERS, SEPTEMBER 11, 2016 (27–23 LOSS)
GAMES: 32 | **TACKLES:** 128 | **INT:** 6 | **TDS:** 1

TRACK AND FIELD STAR

While in high school, Ramsey was a superstar on the football field and the athletics track. A superb sprinter, he also competed at high jump, triple jump, and shot put, but it was as a long jumper and a sprinter that he really excelled. He posted 10.50 seconds for the 100-meter dash and, in his very last high school track meet in May 2013, he broke a 16-year Tennessee state record with a long jump of 25' 3.25". He joined Florida State University later that year, and became the first cornerback to start all 14 games for the Seminoles in their freshman year since Deion "Primetime" Sanders back in 1985.

CORNERBACK KING

Ramsey's first year with the Jaguars was a tough one, as they ended up with a 2–12 record. Even so, he finished with figures of 65 combined tackles (of which 55 were solo), 14 pass deflections, two interceptions, and even scored his only (to date) touchdown. The following season proved a turning point for the Jaguars. With Ramsey at the heart of a reborn defense, the Jaguars finished the season 10–6 and roared through the playoffs, reaching the AFC Championship where they were narrowly defeated 24–20 by the Patriots. Ramsey finished the year with 63 tackles (52 solo), 17 pass deflections, and four interceptions, and was also chosen for his first Pro Bowl.

FIRST-ROUND PICK

During his three-year college career, Ramsey continued to post amazing figures, finishing with 181 tackles, five sacks, and three interceptions from 41 games. He opted out of his senior year, choosing to make himself available for the 2016 NFL Draft where he was expected to be a first-round pick by many NFL experts and scouts. He didn't have to wait long, as the Jaguars stepped in to make him their first choice (and fifth overall). And despite Ramsey requiring knee surgery that summer, Jacksonville offered him a four-year $23.35 million contract, with $22.9 million guaranteed and a signing bonus of $15.18 million. He started paying this back right away, recording three solo tackles in his very first NFL regular season game.

Ramsey dives full-length to stop the charge by Indianapolis tight end, Jack Doyle, in October 2017.

>>>>> FAST FACT >>>>>

In 2015, while still in college, Ramsey posted a long jump of 26' 1.5"–if he'd jumped 3" longer he would have qualified automatically for the U.S. Olympic Team Trials.

JULIO JONES

Julio Jones has everything you need for a good wide receiver— **GREAT SPEED** and a **POWERFUL RUNNING STYLE**. He also has a fantastic pair of hands and an ability to **SOAR INTO THE AIR**, leaving defensive markers quaking at the sight of him.

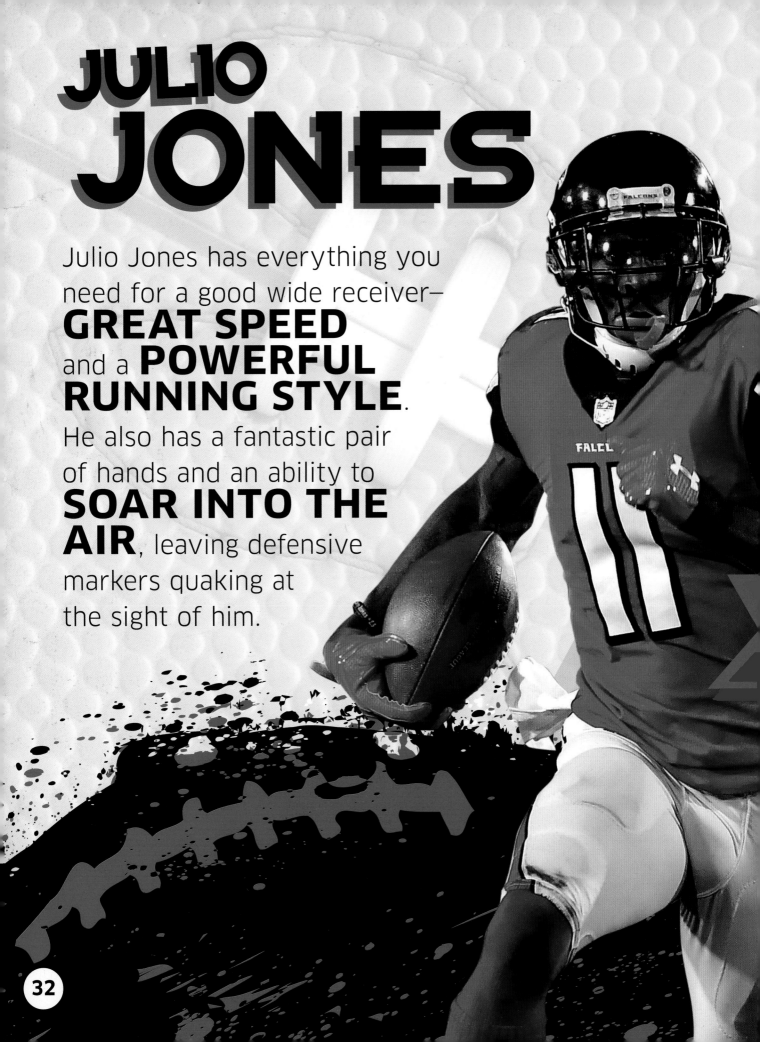

JONES
11

ATLANTA FALCONS | WIDE RECEIVER

D.O.B: FEBRUARY 8, 1989 | **HEIGHT:** 6'3" | **WEIGHT:** 220 LBS
DEBUT: vs. CHICAGO BEARS, SEPTEMBER 11, 2011 (12–30 LOSS)
GAMES: 95 | **RECEPTIONS:** 585 | **YARDS:** 9,054

SCHOOL AND COLLEGE STAR

Whether it was on the football field, the basketball court, or on the athletics track, Jones was an excellent athlete and was even named Mr. Alabama Track and Field Athlete of the Year in 2007. During his junior year in school he caught 75 passes for 1,306 yards, which brought him to the attention of the University of Alabama, which he committed to in 2008 and joined the powerful Crimson Tide team. In college, he soon made a reputation as an impact player. During his junior year, he made 78 catches for 1,133 yards and scored seven touchdowns.

THE NFL

His blazing college form persuaded Jones to give up his final year and he declared himself eligible for the 2011 NFL draft, where he was picked sixth overall by the Falcons. Jones set about tearing through opposition defenses, chewing up the yards and plucking passes out of the air. He helped the Falcons to the playoffs in his rookie year and made the Pro Bowl in his second season. A broken foot saw his 2013 season cut to just five games, but Jones bounced back and in 2015, Atlanta gave him a huge $71.5 million extension to his contract. He paid that back by recording 1,871 yards that year—a Falcons record and the second highest in NFL history, after Calvin Johnson of the Lions.

Jones scores one of his trademark athletic touchdowns against Tampa in November 2017.

>>>>> FAST FACT >>>>>

At the 2011 NFL Scouting Combine, Jones posted the longest long jump and the third-fastest 40-yard dash among wide receivers—all with a broken foot bone.

CATCHING MACHINE

In his seven seasons in the NFL to date, Jones has managed 585 catches in his 95 games for a total of 9,054 yards, averaging more than 95 yards a game for a career total of 43 touchdowns. It's no wonder, then, that he's been chosen for five Pro Bowls and only just missed out on a Super Bowl ring when the Patriots beat the Falcons in overtime at Super Bowl LI in 2017. He finished the 2017 season posting 88 receptions for 1,444 yards at an average of 16.4 yards for three touchdowns.

TYRON SMITH

Big and imposing, Tyron Smith is one enormous **OFFENSIVE WALL**, blocking the defense and **PROTECTING HIS QB**. But don't let his size fool you—he also has incredible **SPEED** and **MOBILITY**, making him one of the best offensive linemen in the NFL today.

SMITH
77

DALLAS COWBOYS | OFFENSIVE TACKLE

D.O.B: DECEMBER 12, 1990 | **HEIGHT:** 6'5" | **WEIGHT:** 320 LBS
DEBUT: vs. NEW YORK JETS, SEPTEMBER 11, 2011 (24–27 LOSS)
GAMES PLAYED: 105 | **GAMES STARTED:** 105

NUMBER ONE PROSPECT

Throughout his high school career, Smith played on both the offensive and defensive lines, earning regional and All-American honors. But it was his performances as a right tackle that drew the most attention, with many analysts and experts rating him as a potential five-star recruit, while Rivals.com called him "an amazing right tackle prospect." Growing up in California, he made an easy choice of USC as his college. Playing as backup left offensive tackle, or starting as right offensive tackle, his performances for the Trojans were good enough for him to win the Morris Trophy for best lineman in the All-Pac-10 Conference.

INTO THE ACTION

The Cowboys wasted little time in picking Smith as part of the first round (9th overall) in the 2011 NFL Draft. Signing him on a four-year $12.5 million contract, they also didn't waste any time in naming him to the starting lineup as right tackle—part of a new-look offensive line. His performances in that rookie season were so good that many people believed he would make the move to the more technically demanding left tackle position. This happened the following year and Smith's performances continued to improve. In the 2013 season, he committed just one holding penalty and allowed only one sack in his 16 starts.

Smith and his fellow offensive team celebrate a touchdown against the Raiders during a 2017 preseason game, which the Cowboys won 24–20.

>>>>> **FAST FACT** >>>>>

In high school *Smith was a top-rated field athlete, and recorded best throws in the shot put of 46'7", and 152'10" in the discus.*

BETTER AND BETTER

Having been named to the 2014 Pro Bowl (his first), the Cowboys offered Smith a huge eight-year $109 million contract extension, making him the highest-paid offensive lineman in the NFL at the time. With Smith in the line, the Cowboys became the NFL's second ranked rushing offense that season, and with Smith blasting holes in opposing defenses, Dallas running back, De Marco Murray, became the top rusher that year. Injuries have hampered him over the last two seasons, but he's still made the Pro Bowl in every season.

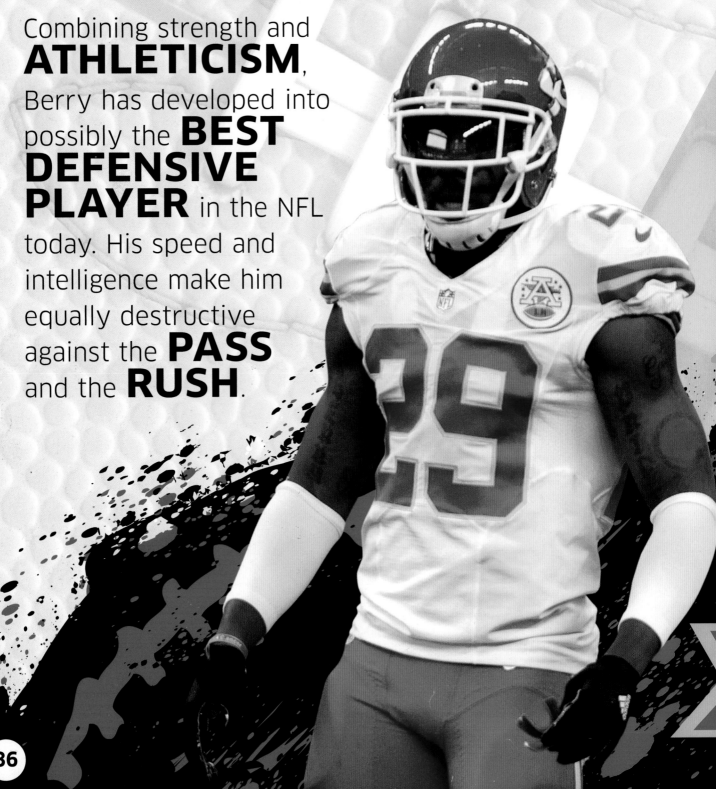

ERIC BERRY

Combining strength and **ATHLETICISM**, Berry has developed into possibly the **BEST DEFENSIVE PLAYER** in the NFL today. His speed and intelligence make him equally destructive against the **PASS** and the **RUSH**.

BERRY
29

KANSAS CITY CHIEFS | SAFETY

D.O.B: DECEMBER 29, 1988 | **HEIGHT:** 6'0" | **WEIGHT:** 212 LBS
DEBUT: vs. SAN DIEGO CHARGERS, SEPTEMBER 13, 2010 (14–21 WIN)
GAMES: 87 | **TACKLES:** 434 | **INT:** 14 | **TDS:** 5

COLLEGE BEST

Berry was a natural athlete in high school, where his superb pace saw him record 21.76 seconds for the 200-meter dash. As a cornerback and quarterback on the football field, he earned a 37–5 win-loss record during his high school career. He chose to attend the University of Tennessee. Right away, Berry made an impact for his new college, forcing his way into a starting position during his freshman year, and being named team captain in his sophomore year. By the time his college career ended, he was a unanimous First-team All-American two years in a row and won the Jim Thorpe Award for the best defensive back in college football.

IMMEDIATE IMPACT

Berry chose not to stay on for his senior year and made himself available for the 2010 NFL Draft. With his college record, Berry was expected to be an early draft choice and the Chiefs made him their top priority, choosing him in the first round and the fifth overall pick. He started all 16 games in his first season with the Chiefs, leading the team in interceptions, and even being selected for the Pro Bowl. In 2014, however, Berry reported a pain in his chest. A growth was found and he was diagnosed with cancer.

BACK WITH A BANG

In July of 2015, Berry anounced that after successful treatment, he was now cancer free. That season he regained his starting position, was chosen for the Pro Bowl again, was named Comeback Player of the Year, and helped the Chiefs clinch a Wild Card spot with an 11–5 record. The following season proved even more successful for Berry as he was selected for his fifth Pro Bowl, his third First-team All-Pro, and was selected as the best defensive back by his fellow players. In recognition of this, the Chiefs offered Berry a huge six-year $78 million deal with $40 million guaranteed and a $20 million signing bonus, making him the highest-paid safety in the NFL.

Berry reaches high to block a pass against the New York Jets in front of a home crowd at Arrowhead Stadium in September 2016.

>>>>> FAST FACT >>>>>

Berry suffers *from equinophobia, or a fear of horses. Which is a bit unlucky as the Chiefs' mascot is Warpaint—a pinto horse!*

DEREK CARR

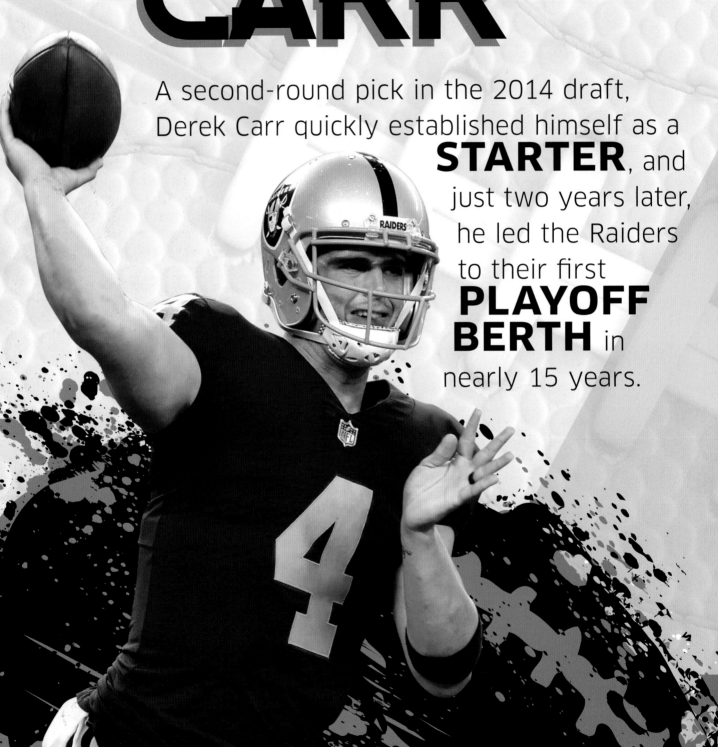

A second-round pick in the 2014 draft, Derek Carr quickly established himself as a **STARTER**, and just two years later, he led the Raiders to their first **PLAYOFF BERTH** in nearly 15 years.

OAKLAND RAIDERS | QUARTERBACK

D.O.B.: MARCH 28, 1991 | **HEIGHT:** 6'3" | **WEIGHT:** 215 LBS
DEBUT: vs. NEW YORK JETS, SEPTEMBER 7, 2014 (14–19 LOSS)
GAMES: 62 | **ATT:** 2,247 | **COMP:** 1,378 | **YARDS:** 14,690 | **TD:** 103

FOOTBALL FAMILY

Carr's pedigree is second to none. His uncle, Lon Boyett, was a tight end who played for the Raiders in the '70s, while his older brother David was a first round draft pick for the Texans in 2002 and had a 10-year career in the NFL that saw him clinch a Super Bowl title with the Giants in 2012. It's no surprise that Carr excelled at football during his school and college years. During the three years he was starting quarterback with the Fresno State Bulldogs, he threw for 12,843 yards and 113 touchdowns. In 2013, he won the Sammy Baugh Trophy, which is awarded to the country's top college quarterback. In honor of his achievements, the college even retired his number 4 shirt, a number he chose to wear out of respect for his favorite player, legendary quarterback Brett Favre.

PRIZE ASSET

Carr hit the ground running in the NFL, setting a Raiders record for the most passing touchdowns in a single regular season game by a rookie, with four against the Chargers in only his fourth game. He quickly became the Raiders' number one quarterback and his performances were rewarded in 2017 with a huge five-year $125 million contract extension, making him one of the league's highest-paid players in terms of average earnings per year. In 2018, he was named to his third straight Pro Bowl.

Carr celebrates another touchdown with wide receiver Amari Cooper against the Kansas City Chiefs in October 2017.

FAST FEET

Carr is renowned for his athleticism and his fast feet can take him out of almost any sort of trouble. He can also deal with pressure when things don't quite go according to plan, rolling out of a pocket or evading the rush of an oncoming defense. And while his long passing may be a weakness, his quick arm can be devastating over short and medium passes, as is his ability to adapt to different systems and catchers with ease.

>>>>> FAST FACT >>>>>

Against the Panthers in 2016, Carr broke the pinkie on his throwing hand, but that didn't stop him leading the Raiders to a 35–32 victory.

DREW BREES

Drew Brees is one of the most **DECORATED** quarterbacks in the NFL today. His list of achievements is as long as they come. Since joining the **SAINTS**, he's led NFL QBs in touchdowns and passing yards. He's also passed for more than **5,000 YARDS** in five different seasons—**NO ONE** else has done this more than once!

NEW ORLEANS SAINTS | QUARTERBACK

D.O.B: JANUARY 15, 1979 | **HEIGHT:** 6'0" | **WEIGHT:** 209 LBS
DEBUT: vs. KANSAS CITY CHIEFS, NOVEMBER 4, 2001 (25–20 LOSS)
GAMES: 249 | **ATT:** 9,294 | **COMP:** 6,222 | **YARDS:** 70,445 | **TDS:** 488

A STAR IS BORN

It's fair to say that Brees had a stellar football career in high school and at Purdue University. During his time with the Boilermakers, he made a name for himself setting records. These included two NCAA records, 13 Big Ten Conference records, and 19 Purdue University records. He also holds the NCAA record (jointly) for the longest pass ever to a receiver of 99 yards. Despite all of these achievements, analysts and experts had their doubts and thought he was a little short for a quarterback and was a bit lacking in arm strength. As a result, he had to wait until the second round and the 32nd pick overall before the Chargers chose him in the 2001 NFL Draft.

FLYING START

Brees made a solid start for the Chargers, working his way into the starting lineup. In 2004, he led the team to a 12–4 regular season record, winning the AFC West for the first time in ten years. But he was never settled with the team and left as a free agent after the 2005 season to join up with the New Orleans Saints. In his first season with the Saints, he guided them to a 10–6 regular season record and then all the way to the NFC Championship game where they were beaten 39–14 by the Bears. But more was to come just three years later.

SUPER BOWL AND BEYOND

In 2009, Brees was at the helm again, passing the Saints to Super Bowl XLIV where they defeated the Colts 31–17, and Brees was named Super Bowl MVP. Since then, he's rolled over record after record, climbing up the quarterback charts and becoming only the third player to have more than 70,000 passing yards (the others being Peyton Manning and Brett Favre), but being the fastest to do so in just 248 games. He even broke a 52-year-old-record held by football legend Johnny Unitas when he threw at least one touchdown pass in 54 consecutive games (Unitas had managed just 47).

Brees passes over the Falcons' defense to wide receiver Michael Thomas during a game in December 2017.

▶▶▶▶▶ FAST FACT ▶▶▶▶▶

More than *16 years after leaving college, Brees still holds Big Ten records in several passing categories, including completions (1,026) and yards (11,792).*

DAVID JOHNSON

He may have only had three seasons in the NFL, but David Johnson has not wasted any time in making a **BIG IMPACT**. Good with his hands and even better on his feet, he's proved himself a **KEY PART** of the Cardinals' offensive plans.

JOHNSON
31

ARIZONA CARDINALS | RUNNING BACK

D.O.B: DECEMBER 16, 1991 | **HEIGHT:** 6'1" | **WEIGHT:** 225 LBS
DEBUT: vs. NEW ORLEANS SAINTS, SEPTEMBER 13, 2015 (31 WIN)
GAMES: 33 | **ATTEMPTS:** 429 | **YARDS:** 1,843 | **TDS:** 24

THREE-SPORT STAR

While at school, Johnson excelled on the football field, basketball court, and the athletics track. On his school basketball team, he averaged 15.7 points and 7.9 rebounds per game, while on the track his speed saw him record 11.03 seconds for the 100-meter dash. But football was his first love and during his senior year, his 42 touchdowns helped his school team to an 11–1 record and earned him a scholarship to the University of Northern Iowa. During his first season playing for the college, he recorded impressive figures, with 179 rushes for 822 yards and nine touchdowns.

RUSHING RECORDS

Johnson continued his good form throughout his college years, peaking during his senior year. During the 2014 season, he made 287 carries for 1,553 yards, scoring 17 rushing touchdowns in the process (he also managed 38 receptions for 536 yards and two touchdowns). He set college records for career yards, career rushing touchdowns, and career all-purpose yards. The Cardinals picked Johnson in the third round of the 2015 NFL Draft as a fourth string running back. First season chances were limited, but Johnson still started five games and scored eight rushing and four receiving touchdowns.

Johnson shows surefooted agility to hurdle Robert McClain of the Carolina Panthers (now with the Buccaneers) during the 2016 season.

>>>>> FAST FACT >>>>>

In the 2016 season, Johnson recorded more receiving yards than any other running back in the NFL, showing just how versatile a player he is.

CUT SHORT

Johnson really shone during his second season with the Cardinals, recording at least 100 yards in 15 straight games, matching the record for the longest single-season streak set by rushing legend Barry Sanders of the Lions. He finished the year ranked seventh for rushing yards (1,239) and second for rushing touchdowns (16). The next season was not as successful. A dislocated wrist in the season opener against the Detroit Lions ruled him out for the rest of the year.

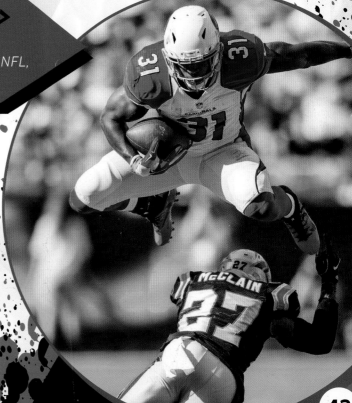

TODD GURLEY

SPEED and **POWER** are two things you're guaranteed with Todd Gurley. And he uses these to great effect, **SMASHING** through any defensive line and brushing off all but the **TOUGHEST OF TACKLES**.

GURLEY II
30

LOS ANGELES RAMS | RUNNING BACK

D.O.B: AUGUST 3, 1994 | **HEIGHT:** 6'1" | **WEIGHT:** 227 LBS
DEBUT: vs. PITTSBURGH STEELERS, SEPTEMBER 27, 2015 (12–6 LOSS)
GAMES: 44 | **ATT:** 786 | **YARDS:** 3,296 | **TDS:** 29

SPEED MACHINE

At school and college, few could keep up with Gurley's raw speed. He was a world class hurdler and sprinter, representing Team USA at the 110-meter hurdles at the 2011 World Youth Championships in Athletics, and posting a career best of 13.66 seconds. He also ran a personal best in the 100-meter dash of 10.70 seconds. It's no surprise then that he was made North Carolina Player of the Year, having posted 2,600 yards and 38 touchdowns in his senior high school year in 2011. Moving to the University of Georgia in 2012, he rushed for 1,385 yards and 17 touchdowns in his freshman year.

THE HARD YARDS

Gurley opted out of his senior year and was picked by the Rams in the first round of the 2015 NFL Draft. He had to ease his way into his rookie season after a knee injury, but was soon up to speed and recorded 566 rushing yards in his first four games. He finished his rookie year with 1,106 rushing yards and ten touchdowns on 229 attempts. His figures were enough to earn him selection to the 2016 Pro Bowl. The following season proved much harder, with the Rams finishing with a 4–12 record and Gurley only posting 885 yards all season.

BACK WITH A BANG

New season, new head coach, and 2017 saw a change in the fortunes of Gurley and the Rams. With Sean McVay as head coach, the Rams ended the regular season with 11–5 and a spot in the playoffs. On the way, Gurley rushed to a total of 1,305 yards from 279 attempts and 13 touchdowns. On top of this, he added 788 yards, receiving yards for six more touchdowns. And he even sat out the final game of the regular season as the Rams rested him for the playoffs! Small wonder he was voted NFL Offensive Player of the Year!

Gurley reaches into the end zone to score against the Philadelphia Eagles in December 2017.

>>>>> FAST FACT >>>>>

During his rookie year in 2015 and following a 27-6 win over the 49ers in Week 8, Gurley's jersey and cleats were inducted into the Pro Football Hall of Fame.

x

HOW WELL DO YOU KNOW THE NFL?

So you think you know all about the NFL's teams, star players, and prospects? Try out this 24-question quiz to test your knowledge and memory. The answers are on page 48, but no peeking before completing the quiz!

1. WIDE RECEIVER, A.J. GREEN, COMPETED IN LONG JUMP AND TRIPLE JUMP AT HIGH SCHOOL. HE ALSO HAD A HOBBY AWAY FROM THE SPORTS FIELD. WHAT WAS IT?
a) Swimming
b) He was in a band
c) Juggling

2. WHICH QUARTERBACK PLAYER WAS OFFERED A CONTRACT TO PLAY MAJOR LEAGUE BASEBALL WITH THE MONTREAL EXPOS, BUT TURNED IT DOWN TO PURSUE FOOTBALL?
a) Tom Brady
b) Matthew Stafford
c) Eli Manning

3. WHICH RAIDERS PLAYER HAD THE HIGH SCHOOL NICKNAME "BOMBSHELL MAN"?
a) Khalil Mack
b) Derek Carr
c) Karl Joseph

4. HOW MANY PRO BOWL APPEARANCES HAS ANTONIO BROWN MADE WITH THE PITTSBURGH STEELERS?
a) 5
b) 6
c) 8

5. WHICH WIDE RECEIVER WAS NAMED THE MR. ALABAMA TRACK AND FIELD ATHLETE OF THE YEAR IN 2007?
a) Julio Jones
b) Antonio Brown
c) A.J. Green

6. IN THE 2015 NFL SEASON OPENER, AARON DONALD RECORDED NINE TACKLES FOR THE RAMS (A CAREER HIGH) AGAINST WHICH TEAM?
a) Washington Redskins
b) Cleveland Browns
c) Seattle Seahawks

7. DURING THE 2018 INTERNATIONAL SERIES IN LONDON, UK, WHO WILL PLAY THE SEAHAWKS?
a) Oakland Raiders
b) Philadelphia Eagles
c) Tennessee Titans

8. FOOTBALL ANALYST, MEL KIPER JR., SAID THAT WHICH YOUNG QUARTERBACK WOULD BE THE "NUMBER ONE PICK IN THE NFL DRAFT" BEFORE HE'D EVEN PLAYED A COLLEGE GAME?
a) Patrick Peterson
b) Trevor Williams
c) Jalen Ramsey

9. WHICH CITY WILL HOST THE SUPER BOWL LIII?
a) New Orleans
b) Atlanta
c) Detroit

10. LUKE KUECHLY WON THE 2011 BUTKUS AWARD FOR BEST COLLEGE LINEBACKER AFTER A SENSATIONAL COLLEGE CAREER. WHICH COLLEGE DID HE PLAY FOR?
a) Texas A&M Aggies
b) Boston College Eagles
c) Alabama Crimson Tide

11. HOW MANY TEAMS MAKE UP THE NFL'S SIX DIVISIONS, COMPETING TO REACH THE NEXT SUPER BOWL?
a) 38
b) 50
c) 32

12. WHICH ARIZONA CARDINALS PLAYER RECORDED AT LEAST 100 YARDS IN 15 GAMES STRAIGHT, MATCHING THE RECORD FOR THE LONGEST SINGLE-SEASON STREAK SET BY BARRY SANDERS?
a) David Johnson
b) Chris Johnson
c) Carson Palmer

13. DREW BREES MOVED TO THE NEW ORLEANS SAINTS FOR THE 2006 SEASON AFTER PLAYING FOR WHICH TEAM BETWEEN 2001 AND 2005?
a) Dallas Cowboys
b) Los Angeles Rams
c) San Diego Chargers

14. HOW MUCH DID THE PITTSBURGH STEELERS OFFER ANTONIO BROWN FOR HIS RECORD-BREAKING FIVE-YEAR CONTRACT?
a) $68m + $19m at signing
b) $58m + $20m at signing
c) $66m + $17m at signing

15. WHICH PHOBIA DOES KANSAS CITY CHIEFS PLAYER, ERIC BERRY, SUFFER FROM?
a) Apiphobia (fear of bees)
b) Equinophobia (fear of horses)
c) Taphophobia (fear of being buried alive)

16. WHICH PLAYER HAS PLAYED IN EVERY SINGLE REGULAR SEASON GAME IN HIS SEVEN SEASONS WITH THE CARDINALS?
a) Patrick Peterson
b) Josh Allen
c) David Johnson

17. BUTKUS AWARD WINNING OUTSIDE LINEBACKER, VON MILLER, GRADUATED IN 2011 WITH A DEGREE IN WHICH SUBJECT?
a) Dairy Science
b) Poultry Science
c) Land Development

18. WHICH TEAM SIGNED TYRON SMITH TO A FOUR-YEAR $12.5 MILLION CONTRACT IN THE 2011 NFL DRAFT?
a) Dallas Cowboys
b) Atlanta Falcons
c) Pittsburgh Steelers

19. WHO SIGNED A $72 MILLION SIX-YEAR CONTRACT IN 2008 DESPITE HAVING NEVER PLAYED A PROFESSIONAL GAME?
a) Drew Brees
b) Carson Wentz
c) Matt Ryan

20. WHICH PLAYER HAS AN UNCLE WHO PLAYED FOR THE OAKLAND RAIDERS IN THE '70s AND AN OLDER BROTHER WHO WON THE SUPER BOWL WITH THE GIANTS IN 2012?
a) T.J. Watt
b) Von Miller
c) Derek Carr

21. WHICH TEAM SIGNED CARSON WENTZ IN THE FIRST ROUND AND SECOND OVERALL FOR THE 2016 NFL DRAFT, WITH A FOUR-YEAR $26.67 MILLION CONTRACT?
a) Philadelphia Eagles
b) New England Patriots
c) Jacksonville Jaguars

22. WHICH PLAYER SPENT THE FIRST THREE YEARS OF HIS NFL CAREER AS AN UNDERSTUDY TO QUARTERBACK, BRETT FAVRE?
a) Tom Brady
b) Aaron Rodgers
c) Khalil Mack

23. WHICH PLAYER'S JERSEY AND CLEATS WERE INDUCTED INTO THE PRO FOOTBALL HALL OF FAME IN HIS ROOKIE YEAR (2015)?
a) Carson Wentz
b) David Johnson
c) Todd Gurley

24. TOM BRADY HAS WON MORE SUPER BOWL RINGS THAN ANY OTHER ACTIVE PLAYER, BUT FOR WHICH TEAM?
a) Kansas City Chiefs
b) New England Patriots
c) Jacksonville Jaguars

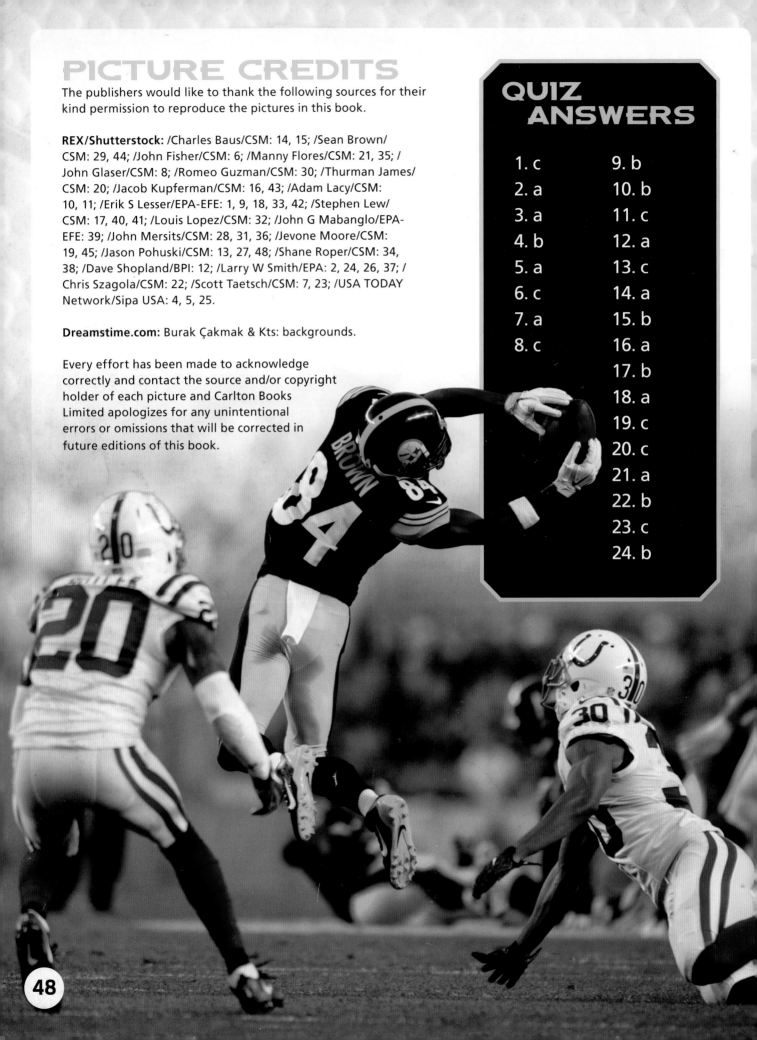

PICTURE CREDITS

QUIZ ANSWERS

1. c	9. b
2. a	10. b
3. a	11. c
4. b	12. a
5. a	13. c
6. c	14. a
7. a	15. b
8. c	16. a
	17. b
	18. a
	19. c
	20. c
	21. a
	22. b
	23. c
	24. b